GOD DID IT!

By
LaTesha Rogers Dorsey

_____

God Did It! By
LaTesha Rogers Dorsey

Published By Parables
April, 2021

All Rights Reserved. No part of this book may be reproduced or utilized in any form or by any means, electronic or mechanical, including photocopying, recording, or by any information storage and retrieval system, without permission in writing from the author.

    Printed in the United States of America

Readers should be aware that Internet Web sites offered as citations and/or sources for further information may have been changed or disappeared between the time this was written and the time it is read.

God Did It!

By
LaTesha Rogers Dorsey

PUBLISHED by PARABLES
Earthly Stories with a Heavenly Meaning

God Did It!

Acknowledgments

*First, I thank God for helping me write this book. I am also thankful for the material that I was able to include about Him.
*I want to thank my mama, Doris A. Addison. Words cannot express the love and support that you gave me in writing my first book. I love you!

*I want to thank my father-Leo J. Rogers, Aunt Wanda P., TIKK, Shon, Dana, and my son-Quentyn. I love all of you!

*I want to thank my husband, Nathaniel Dorsey (Bo) for buying me the laptop where I was able to write my book. Thank you for the love and support that you gave me! Also, thank you for financial support. I love you and I thank God for you!

Special thanks to Bishop Raymond W. Johnson for my healing prayer and material written in this book
**Special thanks to my grandmother, Doris M. Pitts. Thank you for the idea to write a book. Thank you for your love and support. I will always love you Dear!

LaTesha Rogers Dorsey

Preface

One summer morning I was awakened out of my sleep because I had to use the bathroom. I had to pee! However, this morning my toes felt funny. It felt like they were fingers bent backwards. On top of that, I could not walk! I got out of bed with God's help I am sure, and I crawled to the bathroom where I used it successfully. God did it! Later, I told my mama what I was experiencing. She called my primary care physician (PCP) and told her what was going on with me. As expected, she told my mama to bring me in for an evaluation. She referred me to a neurologist after my initial exam. I began seeing a neurologist, Dr. Jon Olson. He could not make a diagnosis until I underwent various tests. I took numerous MRI's and spinal taps for the next five months. Finally, I was diagnosed with Multiple Sclerosis (MS) in December 2003. He told me some details related to MS. I will never forget that he told me that I would have to take a shot every day for the rest of my life! WHAT?!!! I hated needles and I

God Did It!

could not accept that. He shared more info and then he handed me three sample shots. He wanted me to take them home and look over the attached information. Well let me tell you! I am a stubborn lady. As soon as I left Dr. Olson's office, I knew what I would do when I got home. I am a woman of my word so once I made it home, I looked for the outside garbage can, and I put the shots in the trash! I was NOT going to stick myself with a needle!!! No one in my family had this disease. I asked the question how I got this mess! Why me?!

Please keep reading to learn how I dealt with my medical diagnosis of Multiple Sclerosis. You will read about the role that God played in my life then and now. You will see God's goodness and his love for me.

LaTesha Rogers Dorsey

Ch. 1 God Did It!

I have already shared with you readers that I was diagnosed with Multiple Sclerosis. What I am about to share is how good God is and how He answers MY prayers. My mother was a member of Living Faith Christian Center in January 2004. She is still a member under Bishop Raymond W. Johnson. Well one Sunday morning in January, I went to church with my mom. Once inside the church, my mom pointed to an area that she wanted us to sit in. I proceeded to a seat while I watched my mom approach Bishop Johnson. I later learned that she went to discuss my recent diagnosis with him. They did not talk for long because it was time for church to start. My mom came to the empty seat next to me and sat down. Shortly after she joined me, music began, and Bishop Johnson began talking. He greeted everyone under the sound of his voice. Next, the choir began singing. Praise and worship continued for about 30 minutes and Bishop Johnson grabbed the microphone again. I thought that he was ready to begin preaching; however, he had just learned some information about a church member-ME! He said that he had just found out that a member had received some bad news from the doctor. He spoke about things that I had been experiencing, and he asked if the individual that he was talking about was in the house then asked would that person please stand. I knew that he was talking about me, so I stood up. When he saw me standing and asked me to come to the altar for prayer. He told me that he wanted to pray a healing prayer over me. Eagerly I moved out of my seat and I quickly made my way to the altar for prayer. I was doubly blessed that morning because LFCC had a guest pastor from Sydney, Australia in attendance. Bishop Johnson shared some words of encouragement as well as some scriptures from the Bible with me. He asked if I was okay with allowing him and the guest pastor to lay hands on me while he said a healing prayer over me. I told him that I welcomed the prayer. I also lifted my hands to acknowledge receipt of the prayer when he began praying for me. I knew that God was at work in my body! I began to cry, and Bishop finished the prayer. He asked me how I felt? I told him that I felt good. I also told him that God had healed my body! I began to move around and jump to show what God had done for me! I did not know that was just the beginning! I returned to my seat with my mom. I was truly appreciative of what my mom had done for me that morning.

God Did It!

Ch. 2 Life Goes On

Christmas 2002 was special. My then boyfriend of 5 years proposed (Mr. Eubanks)! The proposal was different and totally unexpected. I was in my bed sleeping when he appeared in my room, which awakened me. I questioned how he got in my house and he said that my mama let him in. He also had a videographer in my room. I remember saying that I did not want to be on camera since I had just woken up! Plus, the camera had a bright light that was shining directly in my eyes. I asked if he could turn that off and he did. Next thing I knew, he was down on one knee and began his proposal to me! He said a lot of lovely things and then asked if I would marry him? I said yes!

    I had money in my savings as a result of my student loans from my attendance at Southern University. I paid for my own wedding and honeymoon! I did not ask my daddy or mama for any money. My fiancé and I discussed both the wedding and the honeymoon, and we made the final decision. We married on October 4, 2003. Back to my MS story!
I told you that I hate needles, right?! Well, I am about to share another blessing by God that is related to MS. In 2004, I had an appointment with my neurologist, Dr. Zuckerman. I was in his office skimming through magazines as usual. I saw an interesting advertisement in this magazine. The ad was for Gilenya, an oral pill that was as effective as the injection! This meant that I would no longer have to give myself a shot! Instead, I would take a pill everyday once a day. I asked Dr. Zuckerman why he had not told

me about this pill. He said that it was new and had just come out. He did inform me that the manufacturers of the pill were doing a trial study. He told me that because of my diagnosis I qualified to participate in the study. I agreed because all I had to do was take a pill daily, which would be my normal routine. This meant that I would no longer have to take the dreaded shot! I also learned that a participant in the study would be compensated!!! I could not pass up this opportunity. I would be getting paid to do what I would normally do as an MS patient! Hallelujah I exclaimed! Everything worked out beautifully for me. I was blessed with a couple of hundred bucks ($600) and the pill worked very well. Despite my healing in 2004, my doctor still has me taking Gilenya. He does comment on my improvement frequently. I proudly proclaim that God has healed me, and I boast telling him that is why you see improvements. Unfortunately, I still take annual MRIs just to monitor the disease and its effect on my body. I am pleased to report that there have not been any new lesions on my brain! I do still suffer from fatigue and I cannot walk a straight line. However, people with MS are worse off than me. Some people are wheelchair bound for life. Some people do not have use of their limbs, i.e. arms and legs. Others cannot talk. I do not say that I have MS anymore. I tell people that I was diagnosed with MS in December 2003. I am always told that I do not look like I have MS! I quickly tell 'em about my diagnosis in 2003. They usually ask me what happened. I politely tell them that God Did It! and I smile.

Ch. 3 Birth Of My Son

    My best friend, Kim, called me one morning January 2004. She shared with me the most wonderful news that she was pregnant!!! She informed me that she was due in November. I was thrilled because her child was going to be my godchild! Later during the year, I learned that she was going to give birth to a baby girl—Chloe! I admit that I began to become really antsy about my bestie having a baby. I knew that I was fertile so I decided to get pregnant so that I too would have a baby! I did not tell my then husband about my plans. Like most men, he enjoyed having sex so conception would not be a problem! I just had to decide when I wanted my baby to be born. Once I decided on that date then conception would begin! I did not let too much time pass before I decided on September as the birth month of my child. It was easy choosing September because that is my birth month. My birthday is September 22, and I wanted my baby to be born in my birth month. Thinking back, I was not trying to get pregnant. God is good! He knew what I wanted a child to be born in September 2005. God did it for me! I remember waking up one Sunday morning in November 2004 feeling nauseous. I went to church as usual, but I stopped at the dollar store to buy a pregnancy test after church! I was very anxious to take the test. As soon as I made it home, I went to the bathroom to take the test. After two minutes, I discovered that God had answered my prayer—two lines appeared on the stick!!! I was pregnant! I was so happy. I quickly called Kim to share the news. I told her that she was going to be my baby's godmother! She was happy for me and my husband. Immediately I began searching for my obstetrician (Ob). Since this was my first child, I had no idea about selecting an Ob or more importantly who I would choose as my Ob. I just knew that someone had to deliver my baby when I went into labor. I was blessed because my younger sister, Dana, had given birth to four children before me. I was a late bloomer! She told me the names of several people that I could choose as my Ob. I decided to select Dr. Baehr as my Ob. I called to schedule my first appointment. I was successful in securing my appointment. I was early in my pregnancy, so I had to meet Dr. Baehr. I went to my first appointment alone. I liked Dr. Baehr and decided to keep her as my Ob. Pregnancy is forty weeks, so I kept my scheduled appointments as I began to get bigger and bigger! I did not know the sex of my baby. All I know is that I wanted a girl! I do not remember how far along I was in my pregnancy when I got the ultrasound which revealed the sex of my baby. I think that I was twenty weeks. I do remember going to my appointment. I remember being told to undress and put on the gown. The lab tech told me to lie down on the table. She then told me that she was going to apply some cold gel to my belly. After doing that she used the plastic tool to rub the gel on my womb. She only had to do that a few times before she found my baby in my womb. She pointed to the monitor to show me my baby. I heard my baby's heartbeat for the first time! I was extremely excited. I asked if she knew the baby's sex yet. She had not discovered the news yet. After a few minutes she yelled that she knew the sex of my baby. She asked me if I wanted to know. I said "Yes!" I had shared with the lab tech

God Did It!

that I wanted a girl. She decided to play a trick on me. She was able to type the sex of my baby. She began typing "It's a G…" I began screaming because I thought that I was carrying a girl. The tech stopped typing and said that she was playing. She informed me that I was pregnant with a boy! Initially I was disappointed; however, I was told that my son was healthy and that was all that I wanted to hear her say. She confirmed the due date of September 20, 2005, which is two days before my birthday. I was happy that my child was NOT due on MY birthday, September 22!!! I enjoyed my pregnancy. I took maternity pictures with my son's father (my husband at that time). I compiled a list of songs that I wanted to play in the delivery room. I had those songs put on a cd, which I still have today. I reached out to my cousin who made DVDs. He said that he would create a DVD of my son's birth using the footage that his dad would record when I was giving birth. While I was doing all of this, I remembered that we had not chosen a name for our son. We worked together to find a name for our son and finally decided on Quentyn Isaiah Eubanks (Que). I had a doctor's appointment in September 2005 and my Ob discovered that my son's heart rate was irregular. She said that I needed an emergency C-section! She scheduled the C-section for September 19, 2005. I was scared yet excited to deliver my son. I knew that the big day had finally arrived. My husband grabbed the camcorder, cd, cd player and my bag and we were off to the hospital. I checked in when we arrived at the hospital at 6 am. After a short while, I was put in the room where I would remain until my C-section, which was scheduled to begin at 8 am. The nurse came in my room around 7:30 am and explained that I needed to get my epidural! I was already dressed in my hospital gown, so she set everything up and administered the shot. Immediately after that I was taken to the operating room to have my C-section. The doctor gathered all the necessary equipment and asked me how I felt. When I assured her that I felt fine, the C-section began. The doctor on call began cutting my abdomen and feeling around for my son. When he had found him, then he pulled him out! Normally, the mother would hear her child crying, but not me! I saw them put my son on a nearby table and hitting him in the back trying to get him to cry. After what seemed like a long time, I finally heard Que cry! I was under the anesthesia, but I knew that my son was okay. The nurse finally brought Quentyn to me so that I could see my son. He was so handsome with a head full of dark black hair. His dad and my mom were in the hospital room with me. The nurse cleaned my son up and we were off to my room. The nurse placed Que in my arms, but I could not keep him from sliding down. The nurse took Que from me to prevent an accident and led me back to my room. I remember seeing my grandmother, Doris Pitts. She observed my son as he looked around while people were talking. She later told me that he was looking as though he knew that people were talking to him!

Ch. 4 Not So Happily Ever After

    I was released from the hospital with my newborn son on my birthday, September 22! My husband drove me and my son to my mom's house, which is where I had moved to following a separation of me and his dad. I love my mama! She allowed me to move back home with my newborn son! She did not gripe or fuss. Neither did she cuss me out! How many of your mothers would have showed you love like my mama showed me? I am blessed!

    At only six months old, Que's daddy Mr. Eubanks filed for divorce in March 2006. I never thought he would be so cruel to his only son and me, but he was. I had to be a big girl and suck it up. Life goes on, right?! I started casual dating. It was nothing serious. Besides, I had a new baby to look after! I also had to hire a divorce attorney to represent me in my case. I asked around and learned of Kathleen Wilson. I called her and made an appointment to discuss my case. She agreed to meet with me, and I told her about my soon-to-be-ex. I told her about the infidelity that he committed. I also told her about the two children that he had created while he was my man! She agreed to represent me in court.

    It was not long after he filed for divorce that we had to go to court. Judge Luke Laverne presided over the courtroom for our case. My divorce was clean cut. We did not have any property together. The only thing that we did have together was Quentyn, our son! Judge Laverne inquired about Mr. Eubanks' employment status, which was not a well-paying employer. The judge decided on $210 a month! I was shocked! I was kind of pissed! I knew that we would be fine! Why? God was and still is on MY side!!!

Ch. 5 More Problems Arise

More problems arose for me in 2006! I was laid off from my job at Johnson Controls, Inc. If I knew then what I know now, then I would have fought that decision. I did not think about my disability at the time. I could have gone to HR and explained my disability and I might could have saved my job! Oh well, hindsight is 20/20!

God is great to me because my mama checked the mail and discovered a paycheck from Johnson Controls, Inc. (JCI) for me in May 2006! I was no longer an employee of JCI as of April 2006. I was not at home, so she called me to share the wonderful news. When I finally made it back home, I went straight for the check and found it on the counter. I opened it and discovered that it was a paycheck from Johnson Controls, Inc.

A judgement of divorce was granted in 2008 between me and Mr. Eubanks. When the case was closed, I remembered that he was not ordered to pay me alimony since he had created a child when he was my husband! I do not think that my attorney brought that up while we were in court. I thought about it and quickly brushed it off. I said to myself that he did not have any means of paying me!

LaTesha Rogers Dorsey

Ch.6 Another husband

    I do not remember how I met this guy. I do remember that he was cute, tall and interested in me. We started dating in 2012. I learned a lot about this man BUT he did leave out some pertinent information. For starters, he was married! He would leave his wife and come see me. I let him continue in this foolish ungodly behavior for months. We would often have conversations about his life. I even knew his wife's name, but I do not think she knew mines. Heck, I wonder if she knew about me! I later found out that he suffered a tragic loss of a child at the tender age of thirteen! For confidentiality purposes, I will leave the child's name out of my story. I will also leave his dad's name out too! I will refer to him as Two. His child, a son, developed a rare form of cancer, which would eventually kill him. When he told me this information, I was heartbroken. I remember telling him that he was robbed! I told him that I would help him become a father again by conceiving another child with him. He was happy to hear me say that! We were already sleeping together so we would just take it to another level.

    I remembered that I could not conceive a child because I chose to have an IUD placed in my uterus before we met. I had no idea that I would ever get past my first love, Mr. Eubanks. I finally did, however, and I put things in motion. I had a doctor's appointment with my gynecologist. It was a usual check-up. At the beginning of my appointment I told my doctor that I wanted to remove the IUD. She asked me a lot of questions. I think she was just being nosy! However, I answered her questions and she agreed to remove the IUD. For those readers who may be unfamiliar with an IUD it is an intrauterine device that is a form of birth control. It is highly effective and works very well in preventing pregnancy! I know because I had it inserted for four years before requesting the removal. It was risky removing the IUD because I was no stranger to unprotected sex! I did know better, but I had other things on my mind. I wanted to give my friend another child to make up for the child that he had lost. I did not tell him my plan! I just knew that I wanted to get pregnant by him. I continued dating him. We continued engaging in sex frequently. He never wore a condom, so it was no shock when I missed my period quickly after the removal. I took a home pregnancy test to confirm my suspicion. I was right! I was pregnant for Two! In case you are wondering about my age. At this time, I was thirty-four (34) years old and had a son by my first husband. I quickly told Two that I was pregnant! He was thrilled! We went through the typical routine that a pregnant woman goes through, such as finding an ob-gyn and scheduling appointments. Immediately I purchased some prenatal vitamins and began taking them.

God Did It!

I learned some horrible news at my first ob-gyn appointment. When I shared that I had been diagnosed with multiple sclerosis back in 2003, my Ob told me that I would have a high-risk pregnancy! I asked her what did that mean? She told me that I would have to be in bed majority of the time. That did not bother me because I loved to be in bed! Get your mind out of the gutter because I am talking about my love of sleep! Yes, I did love sex too, but I was focused on my sleeping habit. My parents can vouch for me in what I just said. I have always been in bed. I slept late during the week and weekends too! Some may call that lazy, but I do not care. Call it what you want because I have always loved to sleep or just lounge in the bed.

One afternoon, Two gave me some wonderful news. He told me that he and his wife were filing for divorce. I was glad because that meant he would no longer be committing adultery and the two of us could marry once the divorce finalized! Time continued to pass. I am now twenty weeks pregnant and it is time for my child's gender to be revealed! I really wanted to know! I had sought God and asked for Him to impregnate me with a girl. The time had come. I went to my ultrasound appointment waiting to learn the sex of my child. I did the same thing that I did when I was pregnant with Que. I went to my appointment and checked in. I was put in a room where I undressed and put on the gown. A few minutes passed and then the lab tech came into the room. She gave me the instructions as to what I would do, and she asked if I wanted to know the sex of my child. I smiled and answered "YES!" She also asked what I wanted it to be and I told her that I had prayed for a girl. She said okay then let us look. I followed the same procedure that I had done with Quentyn. I laid back on the table and opened the gown to allow the tech to put the gel-like substance on my womb. She applied the stuff to my womb and began rubbing my womb to locate my child in my tummy. It did not take long to see my baby on the monitor. I smiled and asked if she was able to see my child genitals yet. She said not yet. In about another two minutes I noticed her begin typing on the monitor screen. I was not fooled this time. The lab tech told me, "It's a girl!" I yelled, "Thank you God!" I was beyond happy! I could not wait to give her dad the wonderful news! I thought about calling him on the phone but decided that I wanted to tell him face-to-face. I knew that God had impregnated me with a girl because me and Him have a great relationship! He always my prayers. Not to brag, but I know that I am special because not only does he answer my prayers, but he usually answers them quickly almost immediately!

  I waited. I left the doctor's office around 2 pm. He would be getting off and arrive home in three and a half hours. I was nervous while waiting on the time to pass. I decided to call my best friend, Kim, and give her the news. I did exactly what I said I would do. I called her and told her that I found out the sex of my baby. She asked what is

God Did It!

it? I told her that we would be welcoming another girl to the family! She was happy for me because she had already given birth to two daughters and now was my turn! She asked me if Two knew yet and I told her not yet because I was waiting until he got home from work. She congratulated me and told me to call he once I told Two. I said ok!

At this point I am four months pregnant or sixteen weeks. I know now that I am having a girl. I have one objective on my mind-shopping!!! I was eager to begin building a wardrobe for my daughter. I called my bank to see how much money I had in my account. It was not a whole lot but an extra hundred was a great start! I headed straight to Cortana Mall to see what I could find. I do not remember finding anything on my first shopping trip, but I knew that was the first of many shopping trips!

The time has come for my baby's daddy to get home from work. I was ready to share my exciting news with him. I heard the car door close. Next, I heard the knock at my door. I got up quickly and said hey after letting him in. He was just as excited as I was because as soon as he walked in the house, he asked "so what are we having?" I smiled and told him that we were having a girl. He put a bigger smile on his face when he asked what is your due date? I told him May 15, 2013. I told him that me and the baby were doing fine. I reminded him that the doctor said that it was a high-risk pregnancy. He assured me that he had not forgotten about the risk.

LaTesha Rogers Dorsey

My mom started tripping about her house. I was sick and tired of her questions and her usual reminder that I was living in her house, so I told my friend Two that I wanted to move in with him! I knew that he did not have his own place, but I wanted us to move in together especially since I was carrying his child. He did not object. He told me to look for an apartment that was affordable. I did not mind looking since it was my idea. I asked him how much is too costly to pay for a two-bedroom apartment. He said to just look around and let him know the prices that I found for a nice apartment in a nice area. I got an apartment guide from the store and started my search. It did not take me long to find a suitable apartment. My search led me to Greenwell Plaza Apartments on Greenwell Springs Road. I called and learned there were vacancies in the two-bedroom units. Immediately I called Two and told him what I had found. He said okay. He also told me that we would go inspect the area and the apartment before we make our decision. We went to see the apartment complex that weekend. We went to the office and spoke with the office manager. We told him we wanted a two-bedroom apartment. I spoke up quickly and told him that I wanted a downstairs apartment since I was pregnant. He said that we were in luck because one had just become available! I asked the manager when could we move in? The manager smiled and told us that we could move in after we paid the deposit. I said great! He offered to show us that apartment and we agreed to check it out.

God Did It!

The manager took us on a short ride to the vacant apartment. We hopped out of the cart and followed the manager inside. We examined each bedroom. We continued checking out the bathrooms and living room. We looked at the kitchen and inquired about the washroom. After walking around the entire apartment, we exited it. I told the apartment manager that my friend and I would discuss the apartment and we would get back with him later that same day with our decision.

We left the complex and immediately began discussing our future apartment. I say "future" because I liked what I saw, and I knew that Two also liked it. I started asking Two questions to confirm my thoughts. It did not take me asking many questions before I was able to confirm that he agreed with me! We both liked the apartment and wanted to move in as soon as possible so that is what we did. We decided to move into Greenwell Plaza Apartments in November 2012 during my fourth month of pregnancy.

I had furniture in storage from my first marriage. I was glad to use that furniture so I would no longer have to pay that rental fee. We had to each pack our belongings in order to move into our new apartment. The final step before we could move was to find a truck to rent so that we could move my things from the storage unit into our new apartment.

It was easy getting a rental truck from U-Haul. I called and asked about available dates. I was happy to learn that I could get a truck the upcoming weekend, so I booked it. Two arranged for his friends to help load the rental truck at the storage. I packed me and my son's belongings from my mama's house and took it to my new home. Two packed his belongings too and brought them to our new home. Once moved in our apartment, we enjoyed family time. Two enjoyed spending time with my son, Quentyn (Que) who was now age seven. They played his video game together. Que had a favorite game that he liked to play. I do not know the name of the game. Please forgive me! He taught Two how to play the game and that became the norm for those two guys. I was on bed rest, so I usually stayed in our room in bed watching tv. One day while lounging I remembered that I had not chosen a name for my daughter yet! I had thought about various names, including Autumn, Bryonne, Essence, Keia and Khira. I liked all those choices, but I wanted to give Two a chance to help me decide. I called him to our room. I told him that I was trying to choose a name for our daughter. He proudly said that he wanted her to have some of his name included. The name that he wanted in her name was Jerome! I frowned upon the idea because I did not see how to make that feminine. However, I did not throw the idea out of the window. I thought about it and finally came up with the name Jeromia. True, it is not the prettiest name; however, that was part of her daddy's name and he wanted her to have part of his name in hers. I told him that I wanted her to have some of my name too! My favorite name out of the choices was Khira. I said how about we put "La" in front of Khira? I got creative and decided on La'Khira. I loved the name! Now, look at her entire name- La'Khira Jeromia Gibson! Do you like it? No offense, but I really do not care if you like it or not because I love it! After all, I came up with the name! I told Two what I came up with for our daughter's name and he also liked it! That was confirmation! La'Khira Jeromia Gibson was decided to be our daughter's name. That is what we would tell the staff at the hospital when asked after her birth have I her selected her name. I would gladly smile and tell the employee "Yes!" I would tell the employee that her name is La'Khira Jeromia Gibson. I would also tell the story of how we came up with that name giving credit to both her father and I and include sharing both of our names with the employee.

LaTesha Rogers Dorsey

Ch. 7 Life With Two

Now we only have one thing to do and that is to wait on the arrival of La'Khira. The time is moving right along. Let us skip ahead to January 2013. I am now six months pregnant. My stomach is growing but not that much. I have not gained too much weight either. La'Khira is in my womb however, and she is growing.

Two received some horrible news towards the end of this month. He learned that his grandmother died. Here is the relevance of that information. She would be buried in Pascagoula, MS. Two was going to the services but had to make sure that I would not be left home alone. I called my Aunt Connie and told her what was going on and asked her if I could stay with her while Two was gone. She said of course I could stay at her house, so I packed some clothes and went to her house when Two left. I hung out with my Auntie the first day. On the second day La'Khira started being anxious! We all have heard the phrase "ready or not, here I come!" That is exactly what La'Khira was saying because I started having contractions in my sixth month of pregnancy! At first, I brushed it off. I said to myself it is too early to go into labor! I continued watching tv and then I felt another contraction. I stayed seated after that one. I tried to continue watching tv, but my daughter had other plans for me! The contractions kept coming! I started timing them to know when it was time to go the hospital. I stopped timing the contractions when they were coming regularly. I finally got up and told my auntie that I was early, but it was time to go into the hospital because I was having contractions. Thankfully, she did not question me. Instead, she helped me get my bag and we went to her vehicle and got in. The ride to the hospital was long. She lived about 45 minutes away from the hospital. I did not think that I would go in labor that week, especially since Two was in Mississippi. I might have tried to find someone that lived closer to the hospital to spend the weekend with. Oh well, too late now. We finally made it to the new Woman's Hospital, and we went to the Assessment Center. Once inside I was placed in a bed and I was examined. Shockingly, I was 5 cm dilated! Immediately I was placed in a room. La'Khira was born later a few hours later! Her birthday was January 30, 2013. She was not due until May 15, 2013. She weighed 4 pounds and 1 ounce when she was born. As soon as I could get to a phone, I called her dad. I told Two that I went into labor early and our daughter was born! He was sorry that he was not there with me. I told him that my sister was present at the delivery and she took lots of pictures. He told me that he would come home tomorrow. I said okay!

   He is a man of his word. He was at the hospital the next day. He came to my room, kissed me hello and asked where was our baby? I told him that she was in the NICU since she was premature. I called for a nurse to come to my

God Did It!

room. When she arrived, then I told her this is La'Khira dad. I asked if she could take him to meet our daughter. She said "yes", and he went to meet La'Khira.

Two held La'Khira for the first time when he went to see her in NICU. They shared father/daughter time for a few minutes, and then he returned to my room. He was smiling when he returned. I asked him what did he think? He said that we have a beautiful daughter. I said, yes, we sure do!

LaTesha Rogers Dorsey

Ch. 8 More On La'Khira

Two ended up leaving the hospital for the night only to return the next day to bring me home. I learned that La'Khira could not leave the hospital yet. She had to gain a few more pounds. She was well on the way having gained five pounds already. The doctor must have found a weight gainer formula because they were calling to say that La'Khira was ready to come home! We had everything ready to go get our daughter from the hospital. Two and I went to the hospital expecting to bring La'Khira home, but that devil had to mess things up. We had a car seat but did not have the base that went with it. The car seat was a loaner from a friend who just had a baby. I called to ask about the base and found out that she still had it! I was thinking bad thoughts like why in the hell did you not give us the base knowing it was a required to be on the car seat before we could bring La'Khira home! Two left the hospital to get the base from our friend. He was not gone too long. Before I knew it, he was back with the base. I informed that we had the base. She told me that she needed one of us to connect the base to the car seat and when completed she would bring our daughter and buckle her in the car seat. We could finally leave once La'Khira was properly secured in her car seat. That did not take much longer, and we were leaving the hospital with our daughter then. Two drove us home safely and we were about to bring La'Khira to her room finally. I was eager to bring my daughter home to meet her big brother, Quentyn. He opened the door for us when he heard the keys in the door. He ran straight to Two who was holding his lil' sister. Two put her down so that Que could meet her. He was eight years old and big enough to hold her, so I told him to sit down and I placed her in his lap. He was very happy and wore a huge smile on his face! I was excited too! I had my camera ready to capture the moment. I told Que to look at me and smile. He was happy to do that! I let him continue to hold her for a little while. When I felt like he had enough hold time, I took her and laid her in her crib. I told him that I would let him help me when it was her feeding time in a few hours.

His divorce finalized and we married May 9, 2013. Two then became my second husband! We had a private ceremony at our apartment at Greenwell Plaza. A female ordained minister that lived down the street from my mama, which was also a friend of mine performed the ceremony. Both of my children were present. La'Khira was lying in her car seat watching our ceremony. My son, Que, walked me down the hall to meet my future husband. I walked to my favorite gospel singer Canton Jones' song "I'm Fly!" It was my favorite song. I met Two in front of the minister. She went through the usual marriage vows and before I knew it, she said "you may now kiss the bride!" Two leaned down to kiss me and then it was over.

God Did It!

I was married for a second time. We did not go on a honeymoon for financial reasons plus I had just given birth to La'Khira. We enjoyed being a family almost a month when the unexpected occurred. It was June 4, 2013. Two and I were casually drinking in our apartment. He had a 40 oz, and I had a wine cooler. La'Khira was in the room with us. I think she began to feel left out because everyone was drinking but her! She started crying so I fixed her a bottle and fed her. As usual I burped her and put her in the sleeper. It was around 2 a.m. and Two had to go to work in a few hours. We decided to turn in. I went in our room to bed with La'Khira and Two went to the living room where he was sleeping on the couch. La'Khira had a crib to sleep in; however, she had been sleeping with us since we brought her home from the hospital. I know that goes against the sleeping rules, but I missed my babygirl and I was happy to have her home! Her daddy missed her too. He came in the room while we were sleeping, and he took her out of the bed with me. He took her to the living room with him. He put my baby girl on the couch and he also got on the couch. I was sleep so I do not know how they slept. At first guess I thought he put her on his chest and went to sleep. I wish he had not done that. Hell, I wish he would have left her in the bed with me. I heard Two come in the room before he left for work. He did his usual routine with our daughter. He always poked her and said, "good morning nunu." She did nothing so he poked her again and when she did not respond again, he picked her up. He later told me that her lips were blue. I remember that he yelled, "Tesha our daughter is dead!" I woke up out of my sleep when he yelled those words. I remember screaming "Noooooo!" He told me to call 911 but I could not move. He had taken our lifeless daughter in the kitchen and laid her on the counter to perform CPR. That attempt at CPR was unsuccessful! The ambulance arrived and the EMTs came inside. They attempted to revive La'Khira, but they were also unsuccessful, so they took her to the hospital. Her dad and I followed the ambulance to the hospital's emergency room. We went inside to the waiting room while doctors worked on La'Khira in the ER. I do not know how much time had passed but I saw the doctor come into the waiting room where we seated. I saw him drop his head and he came over and said that there was nothing else that they could do. He apologized and told us that she was gone! Again, I screamed and cried! Two grabbed me and held me trying to comfort me. I stood in disbelief! My baby girl was dead! I prayed and asked God to bless me when I was scheduled for my ultrasound to find out the sex of my child. I prayed for a babygirl and God answered my prayer. I told you how I acted in the doctor's office when I was told that I was carrying a girl. I left out pertinent information related to La'Khira's death. The coroner came out and took notes about her death. Her death was ruled accidental due to asphyxiation, which means that she suffocated. It turns out that her dad rolled over on her and she suffocated to death. The coroner also wrote in the report that her ribs had been crushed! Just thinking about her death brings tears to my eyes. I feel bad because my babygirl needed me, but I was sleeping when she lost her life. If only she had been sleeping in her crib, she may still be alive! I tell any expectant mother NOT to sleep with her baby or allow anyone else to sleep with her baby!

   We buried La'Khira exactly one week following her death. I never imagined being in this situation. Hopefully, you have not had to bury your child! Trust me this is a hard pill to swallow! It has been seven years since I lost my daughter and I still have not swallowed that pill!!! The good news is that God has always been with me. His Word is true because it says that He will never leave you or forsake you (Deuteronomy 31:6). Trusting God is how I survived losing my babygirl. We went to the funeral home for the funeral. I broke down when I saw her in the casket. I wanted to pick her up out of the casket. She should not be lying in there! Not MY babygirl! I am a photographer and I bring my camera with me everywhere. Of course, I had my camera with me at La'Khira's funeral. I took a lot of pictures of my babygirl in her casket. There was one thing that I did not like and that is that my daughter's hair was not right! They slicked her hair down and that was ugly! I said to myself why did someone do that to her hair? That style was not cute on my daughter. I continued taking pictures anyway. My child is buried in Clinton, LA where my grandparents are buried. We had to leave the funeral home to take that hour drive. The people who worked at the funeral home came in the room and told us that it was time to load the casket in the hearse. They came to get the casket and put it in the hearse. I cried as they wheeled my babygirl out of the funeral home. They put her casket in the hearse and they drove away headed to Clinton, LA. About an hour later we arrived at Clear Creek Church graveyard where La'Khira is buried. We had a short graveside funeral and then the burial. At her funeral, they lowered her casket in the ground and I thought about jumping in with the casket. I quickly rebuked that devil because I knew that I would not survive if I were buried alive! God brought me back to my senses. The services ended and we returned home to start our lives without La'Khira!

    Guilt was weighing heavily on Two. At home he started crying two days after we buried La'Khira. I questioned him and he told me that he missed our daughter! I told him that I missed her too! A few days passed and Two showed his ass. We were arguing about something and he ended up saying that I killed our daughter!!! I cursed him out! I told him that he is a ******* I told him that there is no way that I killed our daughter. I asked him how in the hell could I crush her ribs? I reminded him that she was sleeping with him. Not to mention he is the one who could have easily crushed her ribs since he weighed 250 pounds! I said if you ever say that again I WILL divorce you! He must have thought that I was playing because on another occasion he messed up and repeated the same BS! I did not tell him what I was going to do. I would just show him. He would know when he was being served!

One night I was watching tv and I saw a legal aid commercial. The narrator asked, "do you want to get a divorce?" I remember saying "hell yes!" I grabbed paper and a pen and wrote down the contact information. I called to obtain the information on how to get a divorce. I got all the information necessary to file for divorce. I do not recall exactly what I had to do to divorce Two; however, I took the necessary steps to end our marriage. I remember I had to pay $250. I do not remember the other steps I had to take to end my marriage. All that matters is that I did everything that I needed to do to end my marriage to Two!

LaTesha Rogers Dorsey

God Did It!

Ch. 9 My God Send

After I divorced Two, I remained single for three years. The summer of 2016 brought about change and it all started with a decision ride the bus to the Belle of Baton Rouge Casino. I did not have a car anymore since I had sold my car to my nephew who needed transportation to get to LSU's campus where he was a beginning freshman. His parents had been looking for a cheap vehicle for a few months. They had not found anything, and school was about to start in a few weeks. My sister and I were talking one day, and she told me that they were having trouble finding an affordable vehicle for my nephew. I asked her how much they were trying to spend, and she said $1800. God had to be on her side because I offered to sell her my car that I was unable to drive my car due to problems as a result of MS. I had a 2009 Mitsubishi Galant that was worth $3000 but I was not gonna deprive my nephew from going to college especially since I had gone to college and earned two degrees. I have a BS in Marketing and an MBA. I wanted to give him the same opportunity that I had. Back to my story! I was sitting at the bus stop when this car pulled up next to the bench and the driver started beckoning for me to come talk to him. He was in the street, so I got up to talk to him. I leaned in the car and spoke to him. He introduced himself as Bo. I told him that my name is Tesha. He asked if I wanted him to take me somewhere. I told him that I was waiting for the bus. He said that he could take me. I asked him if he was a rapist or serial killer? I know you are saying "like he would tell you if he was either of the choices!" He started laughing and told me "no!" I said ok and got in his car. I love music so out of habit I reached over and put the radio on 94.1. He did not say anything when I changed his radio station. He asked me where I was going. I told him that I was going to the Belle of Baton Rouge Casino. I told him that I did not have a lot of money so I would only be about an hour. He said "cool." He continued driving me downtown to the casino. We pulled up to the casino and he asked if I wanted him to come back to get me. I said "yes", and he gave me his number. He said to call him when I was ready to be picked up. I said "okay" and got out of his car. Things did not go well for me at the casino. I lost my $20! Lol. I did not take much to gamble. I was hoping for an increase, but that did not happen! I called Bo to come get me. He showed up quickly and we were on our way. He took me straight home, which is what I wanted him to do that night. I gave him my address and he took me straight there. When we got to my house, he said bye and told me that he would call me tomorrow. I said, "thanks for the ride and okay." I also told him goodnight and I got out of his car. We began conversing daily on the phone. He took me out on dates frequently. This occurred in the summer of 2016. Things were going great between us. He would pick me up and bring me to his FEMA trailer to hang out. We were casually dating! In case you are wondering, yes, we were having sex regularly. I began to feel convicted about having sex with him and we were not married so I told him. I said, "Bo we cannot continue having sex and we are not married!" Bo was

God Did It!

really feeling me! Let me tell you how much he was feeling me. In November 2016, I was at his trailer. I was in his room watching tv. He left me there to go handle some business. When he got back to the trailer, he came to his room where I was watching tv. He handed me a bag. I asked, "what is this?" He told me to look inside the bag. So, I did what he told me to do and I found a beautiful sapphire and diamond ring. Sapphire is my birthstone. He told me that was my engagement ring! I was surprised! I told him that he needed to get down one his knee and ask me to marry him if he was proposing to me. He did what I told him. Bo got down on one knee and asked me to marry him. I said "yes!" I was engaged four months after meeting him! We ended up getting married on September 15, 2018. Our ceremony was held at Life Tabernacle Church led by Pastor Anthony Spell. It was a justice of the peace style ceremony. I only had one attendant, which was my grandmother, Doris Pitts. I am very close to my grandmother. It has been that way since I was a toddler. I would cry just to be with her. If my mom would leave me with my dad's mother, Mrs. Rogers, then I would cry! She began calling my mom's mama to come get me because I would be crying. That episode became my routine. My mama would have to go to work, and she would drop me off at my grandmother's house, Mrs. Rogers, along with my other two sisters. Shon and Dana would be content but not me. I would start crying and not stop until my other grandmother would come get me! Some might call me spoiled but I just call it loved! My grandmother and I are forty years apart! When I was two, then she was forty-two years old. I am currently forty-two, so my grandmother is eighty-two years old! I am so thankful to God that she is still alive and doing well. We are very close, and we still share a close bond. We have a tight relationship! Our close relationship is known by other family members. My husband even knows about my closeness with my grandmother! Speaking of my husband, I am going to get back to my love story about me and Bo. We are going strong in our marriage. We celebrated our two-year anniversary on September 15, 2020! We did not go anywhere because of the Corona Virus b/k/a Covid-19. Things are out of control thanks to this disease. There are millions of people who have contracted this disease and hundreds of thousands have died as a result of this disease. We desire to go to Las Vegas, but that trip is on hold due to Covid-19.

Ch. 10 Life As LaTesha Rogers Dorsey

When I look back over my life, I see just how good God has been and still is to me! He has healed me of a fatal disease that could have killed me, He helped me out of two failed marriages and led me to a man who became my third and final husband! He has helped me not to have financial problems. I hired an attorney in 2008 to help me to get Social Security Disability. I was represented by my Attorney Adam Meunier. Working with him, I was awarded Social Security Disability, which paid me over $1400 per month. My son received a check because he is MY child. His first check was over $400, which is good free money. Both of our pay has increased since it is twelve years later. Que now receives over $1000 per month. I receive over $1700 per month. I am blessed because I do not have to get up for work during the week or on the weekend. I get to sleep until I want to get up except for Sunday mornings. I want to wake up for church. Thanks to Covid-19, I do not go to a church building. Instead, I watch Bishop Gary Hawkins or Pastor Lynwood Spell on my laptop. I love it! I get the Word while lounging in my pajamas. I love being able to hear God's Word being preached every Sunday and Wednesday for bible study. I look forward to things returning to normal. God is waiting on us. The scripture found in 2 Chronicles 7:14 tells us what we need to do if we want God to heal our land: if my people who are called by my name, will humble themselves and pray and seek my face and turn from their wicked ways, then I will hear from heaven, and I will forgive their sin and will heal their land. Give it a try and you will also be able to say God Did It!

About The Author

LaTesha Rogers Dorsey
BS Marketing 2000
Southern University A & M College
Baton Rouge, Louisiana
MBA 2003
Southeastern Louisiana University
Hammond, Louisiana

LaTesha Rogers Dorsey

God Did It!